Linnaeus: Organising Nature

Written by Liz Miles
Illustrated by Jim Mitchell

Contents

Introduction

Who was Linnaeus?

Carl Linnaeus was a brilliant scientist, whose work changed the way people understood **natural history** forever. He had a huge ambition: to study the whole world of plants and animals.

Although he lived over 200 years ago, Linnaeus led the way in developing new ideas that most people still accept today. He's said to be one of the founders of ecology – the study of how animals and plants are connected with each other and with their environments. He understood the links between creatures and their surroundings before the word "ecology" even existed.

Why we still remember Linnaeus today

The main reason Linnaeus is famous today is because of his work as a taxonomist. Taxonomy means studying plants or animals and putting them into groups. It's also known as **classification**. Linnaeus worked out an easy system for classifying plants, and he also made important changes to how animals were classified.

Linnaeus's system made it easier for people to understand the vast plant kingdom, and give sensible names to newly discovered plants. Scientists today still use a classification system that is based on Linnaeus's work.

Wonder in all things

One of Linnaeus's favourite sayings was: "Find wonder in all things, even the most **commonplace**." Linnaeus found wonder in every kind of plant, and in animals too. His love of nature influenced everything he did – teaching, writing, collecting and exploring, as well as science and medicine.

Linnaeus inspecting a *Linnaea borealis*, one of his favourite flowers, which was named after him

Early life

Carl Linnaeus was born on 23 May 1707, in a cottage at Råshult in southern Sweden.

In the early 1700s, this part of Sweden was very similar to how it is today. Forests covered much of the land. Most of the soil was rocky and sandy, so it was difficult to use for growing crops. Further south and on lake shores, where the soil was better, farmers grew crops, such as cereals. Peasants and farmworkers lived in simple wooden houses with **turf** roofs. The wood was from the forest trees, and the turf was cut from the land around.

Most people were poor peasants, living off the land as best they could, using the wood of the forest and rearing animals such as goats. There were few schools, and few children even went to school. There were no laws saying that children had to be educated.

Carl's family was better off than most in Sweden. For generations, many of the men in his family had been farmers or priests. His grandfather was a wealthy farmer, and his father was able to go to university, which only well-off families could afford. Carl's mother was the daughter of a vicar. Carl was the oldest child in the family – he had three younger sisters (Anna, Sophia and Emerentia) and a younger brother (Samuel).

When Carl was two, his father, Nils Linnaeus, became priest at nearby Stenbrohult, and the family moved there, to live by the church. Carl later described it as one of the most beautiful places in Sweden. It was beside a clear-water lake, with surrounding woods of oak, flower-filled meadows and fields growing crops such as hops for beer, and flax for textiles and oil. A ridge of high mountains stood in the distance. The unspoilt countryside was full of wild flowers and birdsong. It was a safe and peaceful place where Carl could play outdoors with his brother and sisters. The nearest town was only about 48 kilometres away, but that was a long journey at a time when trains and cars didn't exist. The only way to travel was by horse, horse-drawn coaches, or walking.

A love of plants

Nils was a keen gardener. Sometimes, he carried his baby son into the garden, lay him on the ground, and gave him a flower to play with. When Carl was four years old, his father took him on a picnic by the lake. Carl listened to Nils tell the guests about the flowers and plants, and how every plant had a name. From then on, Carl was fascinated by plant names. He kept pestering his father to tell him more names.

School days

Carl's father, Nils, taught him a lot, but when he was seven years old, his parents employed a local man called Johan to tutor him at home properly. Only wealthier families could afford tutors, and there were few tutors available. In the early 1700s, only about a third of people in Sweden could read or write. Carl didn't like his bad-tempered tutor, and the garden outside was a big temptation for him to run away from his books. Because Nils loved the garden too, he often took Carl's side when his son chose to explore plants rather than study arithmetic or grammar.

However, Carl's mother wanted him to grow up to be a priest, so he needed to get a good education. The only answer was to send him away to school. When Carl was ten years old, he went to a grammar school in Växjö, a country town 48 kilometres away. His family found it difficult to afford the cost of sending him to school – even the uniform was expensive!

At school, Carl found it hard to concentrate on work. Years later, he remembered that the teachers' strictness made the boys' "hair stand on end".

As he grew older and was given more freedom at school, Carl often played truant, escaping classes in subjects like Latin. He ran away to look for flowers down country lanes and in nearby fields. The other boys at school nicknamed him "the little **botanist**".

Problems at school

By the time he was 15, Carl was in the top class at school and managed to pass a test to get into the next level of education, called the gymnasium. Here, he had to study subjects like Ancient Greek and **Theology** that would lead to him becoming a priest – the career his parents had planned for him. But he was no good at these subjects, and he didn't want to be a priest. He was very good at other subjects, such as Maths and Physics, and had learnt to speak Latin fluently.

When Carl was 19 years old – a year before he was due to go to university to become a priest – Carl's father Nils went to his school in Växjö to check his progress. The teachers explained that Carl was no good at "book-learning" and should be an apprentice to a craftsman, such as a carpenter, instead. Nils was shocked and upset because, at the time, being a priest was seen as a better career. Carl felt bad because he knew that the family had given up a lot to pay for his schooling.

A change of plan

However, one of Carl's teachers, a medical doctor called Johan Rothman, noticed Carl was interested in medicine. He'd begun to play "doctor" with his siblings during school holidays, pretending to treat imaginary illnesses, and mixing medicines from herbs. So Dr Rothman suggested that Carl might study to become a doctor.

At that time, being a doctor was considered lower in status than being a priest, but Nils agreed. Carl was delighted, because in those days, doctors often made their own medicines from plants, so studying Medicine meant studying plants, too.

However, Carl's mother, Christina, was so keen for Carl to be a priest that he was frightened to tell her that he was going into medicine instead. He kept it a secret. In the end, his father told her. But it took even him a year to gather the courage to tell his wife.

Christina's concern was that medicine was less secure, and might not earn Carl a good living. She was right in a way, because at times Carl went on to face poverty as a doctor. Christina was also upset as he was breaking from a family tradition. Although she was always concerned about his choice of career, their relationship was very strong, and when Christina died years later, Carl was grief-stricken.

Linnaeus the student

While Carl Linnaeus was finishing his school studies, Dr Rothman taught him about **botany**. The doctor treated Linnaeus like a son, and knew how intelligent he was. He taught Linnaeus to classify plants using a system developed by a French botanist. This system was based on the structure of the flowers and fruit of plants. Linnaeus tested out the system, and noticed it didn't work for certain plants. This started a thought process that led him to develop his new system of plant classification, called *Systema Naturae*, which was published just nine years after he left school, in 1735.

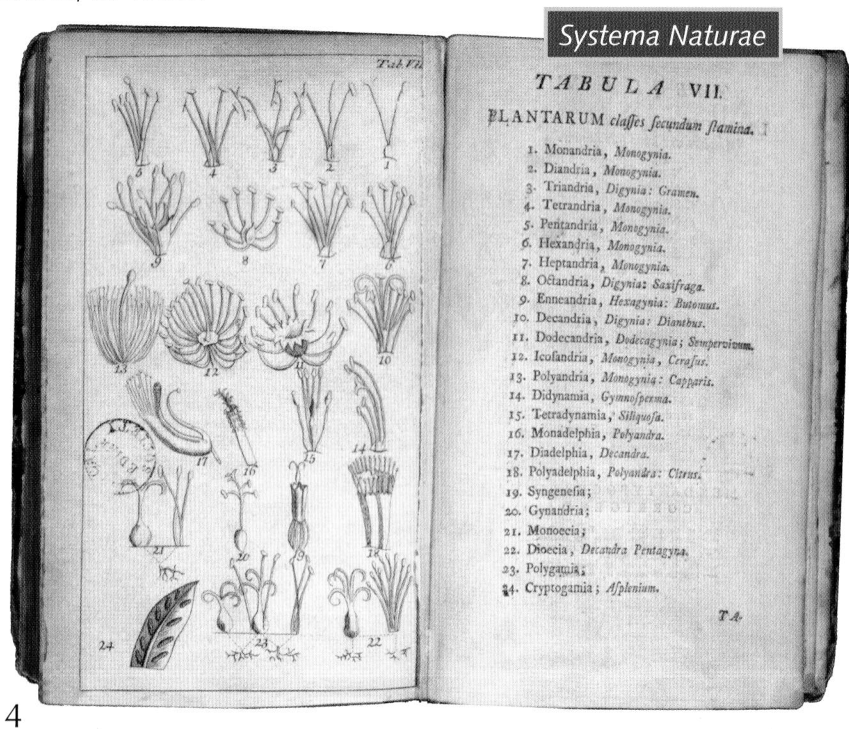
TAB. VII.

TABULA VII.

PLANTARUM *classes secundum stamina.*

1. Monandria, *Monogynia.*
2. Diandria, *Monogynia.*
3. Triandria, *Digynia: Gramen.*
4. Tetrandria, *Monogynia.*
5. Pentandria, *Monogynia.*
6. Hexandria, *Monogynia.*
7. Heptandria, *Monogynia.*
8. Octandria, *Digynia: Saxifraga.*
9. Enneandria, *Hexagynia: Butomus.*
10. Decandria, *Digynia: Dianthus.*
11. Dodecandria, *Dodecagynia; Sempervivum.*
12. Icosandria, *Monogynia, Cerasus.*
13. Polyandria, *Monogynia: Capparis.*
14. Didynamia, *Gymnosperma.*
15. Tetradynamia, *Siliquosa.*
16. Monadelphia, *Polyandra.*
17. Diadelphia, *Decandra.*
18. Polyadelphia, *Polyandra: Citrus.*
19. Syngenesia;
20. Gynandria;
21. Monoecia;
22. Dioecia, *Decandra Pentagyna.*
23. Polygamia;
24. Cryptogamia; *Asplenium.*

TA-

Systema Naturae

In August 1727, Linnaeus went to Lund University. He chose Lund partly because his father had been a student there. Another reason for choosing the university was because it was known to teach Medicine and Botany.

Linnaeus wasn't sure what Lund University would be like. Travel was too difficult to check a university beforehand, and there were no university prospectuses or websites in those days, of course. When Linnaeus arrived, he was very disappointed. He discovered that the university had been neglected. This neglect was partly because Sweden had been involved in expensive wars. There was no money left to give to universities like Lund. Linnaeus found that there was no up-to-date equipment in the Medicine department, and there wasn't even a teacher of Botany.

Lund University, Sweden

University life

Linnaeus went to the lectures on Medicine, but thought he wouldn't stay long on the course. He rented a room in the house of a local doctor called Stobaeus, who studied natural history. Luckily Linnaeus was allowed to study the doctor's impressive collection of rocks, shells and plants. But he wasn't allowed in the doctor's library – it was always locked to protect the valuable books.

Another lodger, who *was* allowed in the library, sneaked natural history books out for Linnaeus to read. One night, Stobaeus found Linnaeus had been up all night, secretly reading his books. From then on, he admired Linnaeus and gave him the library key. He even started giving him free meals, too.

In 1729, Linnaeus moved to Uppsala University, where he'd heard there was a good school of Medicine, and also a **botanical garden**.

Uppsala University, Sweden

More disappointment

When Linnaeus arrived at Uppsala, he found that, like Lund, it was in financial trouble. Again, he was very disappointed. The botanical garden was neglected and the university hospital was poorly run. Worse still, there was hardly any teaching. The lecturer of Botany, Olof Rudbeck, had been given permission to give up lecturing so he could work on his own research. The elderly medical lecturer, Lars Roberg, just wanted to make money on private teaching, and rarely gave university lectures.

Roberg did teach Linnaeus some Botany, and Linnaeus spent a lot of time as a student collecting and studying plants. But he soon began to run out of money. Students often earned money by coaching people on their subject. But Linnaeus couldn't do this because at the time Medicine and Botany weren't popular subjects. He became so poor, he had to replace the worn soles of his shoes with paper.

A *new friend*

Luckily, happier times were coming for Linnaeus. He met Peter Artedi, a clever student who also loved natural history. Together, they decided to study and classify the whole of the plant and animal kingdoms. They divided up the work, Linnaeus taking on most of the plant family, and birds and insects from the animal kingdom. Artedi would do the rest.

A lucky meeting

Olof Celsius

Linnaeus met a second friend in the Uppsala botanical gardens. An elderly clergyman started chatting with Linnaeus about the plants. Linnaeus told him the plant names and how he had a collection of 600 dried wildflowers. The elderly man was very impressed. He turned out to be Olof Celsius, professor of Theology and **dean** of Uppsala Cathedral. Seeing how hungry Linnaeus was, Celsius gave him a room in his house, free meals and the use of his library.

At this time, Linnaeus got a scholarship, which meant he was awarded money. He started work, writing a **thesis** on a subject he was studying – **pollination** in plants.

Pollination

Linnaeus focused on the importance of studying the pollination of plants. He wrote about "male" and "female" parts of plants. He showed the importance of the male stamens and female pistils in creating seeds.

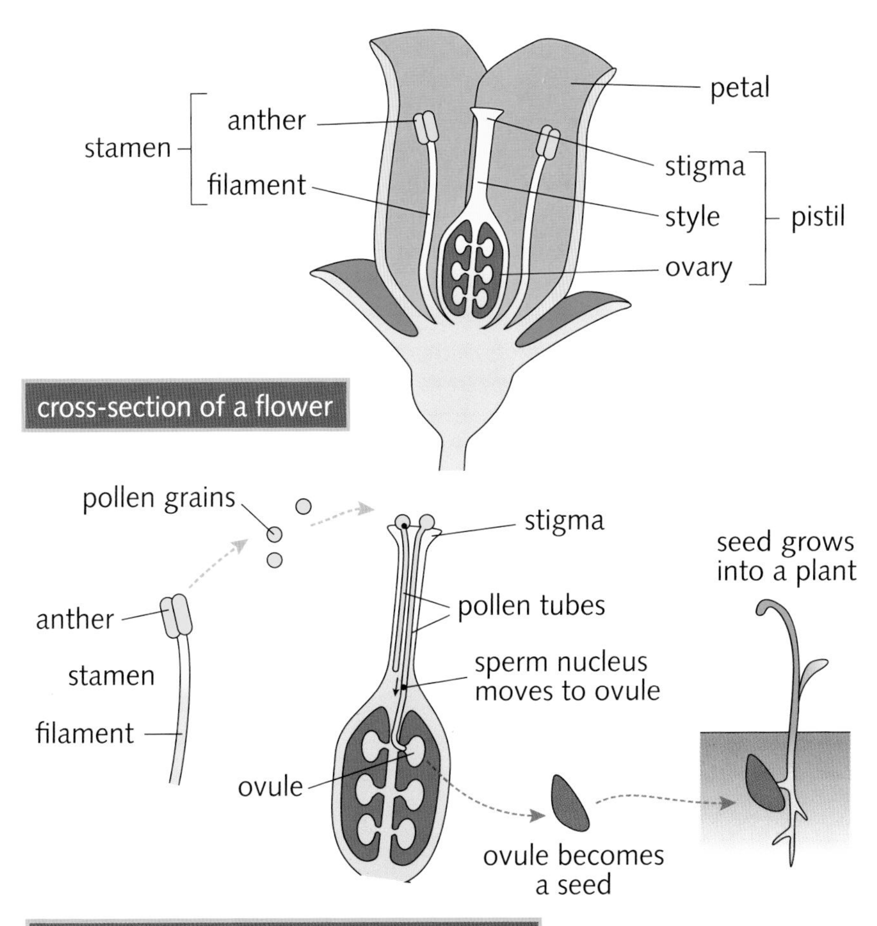

cross-section of a flower

For a seed to grow, pollen must pass from a male anther to a female stigma.

A passion for plants

The language in Linnaeus's thesis showed his passion for plants. His writing is full of enthusiasm and imagery. On the first pages, he describes the beginning of spring.

"In spring ... See how every bird, all the long winter silent, bursts into song! See how all the insects come forth from their hiding-places where they have lain half dead, how the plants push through the soil ... Words cannot express the joy that the sun brings to all living things."

Linnaeus dedicated his thesis to Celsius. Celsius was very pleased with the work and showed it to Rudbeck. The thesis interested lots of people as it was so unusual. Rudbeck was so impressed that he gave Linnaeus the job of giving important spring lectures in Botany in the botanical gardens. Usually, Rudbeck gave the lectures, so people were fascinated to hear that they were going to be done by Linnaeus, still only a second-year student. Rudbeck also asked Linnaeus to move into his home to tutor three of his sons.

When Linnaeus gave his first public lecture that spring in 1730, he was just 22 years old. Soon he was drawing crowds of 300 to 400 people, fascinated by the young man's new ideas and passion!

Linnaeus's naming system

In 1730, while he was still at Uppsala, Linnaeus developed his own system for classifying first plants and then animals. He and Artedi shared their work and discoveries at first, but later lost touch with each other for a few years. Linnaeus's first book about the classification of plants and animals was published in 1735, but he carried on developing it all his life. His classification and naming system helped to change the way scientists looked at and talked about plants and animals forever. We still use parts of his system today.

Why Linnaeus's naming system was needed

Before Linnaeus's system of naming plants, there were no rules. Scientists named plants in the way they chose. One plant could have several names, and the names were often long, describing each bit of the plant.

Linnaeus used just two words to name a plant. The first name was the genus (or group) that the plant belonged to. The second name was the species (or type) within that group. Using this method, he worked out a two-word name for a wildflower that had an eight-word name before.

Linnaeus named this plant *Viola mirabilis*. *Viola* was the genus or group; *mirabilis* was the species or type of Viola. Its old name was far harder to remember or write down: *Viola floribus radicalibus corollatis abortientibus caulinis apetalis seminiferis*.

How Linnaeus's system works

Linnaeus's two-word system of naming followed these steps:

- studying a plant and comparing it with other plants;
- putting the plant into a group of related plants, in order to work out the plant's genus – which becomes the first part of its name;
- identifying a special feature of the plant – this becomes the plant's species, the second part of its name. This second name is like an adjective, describing the plant.

In *Viola mirabilis*, "mirabilis" means wonderful. Today more than 500 species of Viola have been identified and each has its own "binomial name", which means a name with two words.

Linnaeus developed his plant-naming system into a clear method for classifying the whole natural world. He split nature into three kingdoms: animals, plants and **minerals**. He split the kingdoms up into five smaller ranks – first "class", then "order", then "family", then "genus" and finally "species". The genus and species were used to create the binomial name. Some binomial names for animals are used in everyday language now, such as *Tyrannosaurus rex*. Linnaeus was also the first to label human beings *Homo sapiens*.

Gradually, lots of extra layers, such as suborders and subfamilies, have been added to animal classifications. Today, 22 ranks are used in the classification of the leopard. The whole natural world is now divided into five or six kingdoms, and not just the three that Linnaeus used.

This is how Linnaeus classified the leopard:
Panthera pardus (leopard)

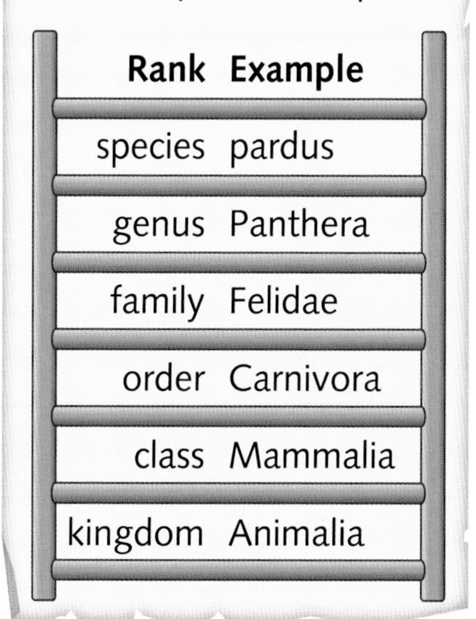

Rank	Example
species	pardus
genus	Panthera
family	Felidae
order	Carnivora
class	Mammalia
kingdom	Animalia

Linnaeus the explorer

Expedition to Lapland

In Linnaeus's time, people rarely travelled to the northern parts of Sweden, Norway and Finland, known as Lapland. It was seen as a mysterious wilderness, where people lived very different **nomadic** lives and spoke an unfamiliar language. But Linnaeus longed to go to Lapland to find out about the plants that grew in the cold climate, and learn more about the people.

Lapland in about 1847

Linnaeus knew that exploring Lapland's wildlife and its people would help his career. But he could only go if he could get a grant from the Royal Society of Uppsala. He put in a request, explaining how important it was to explore the area's rich wildlife and suggesting that he might discover valuable minerals that would help make Sweden rich.

On a visit home, he told his parents of his plans. His mother was worried because so few travellers had visited the area before. She hoped Linnaeus wouldn't get the grant. However, his father understood that the trek could be an important step in his career.

Linnaeus was thrilled when he got the grant in 1732. He excitedly packed the things he needed for the expedition. At that time, there were no lightweight tents or special clothes for crossing mountains and snow-covered forests. His transport was a horse.

Linnaeus's list for the expedition

a coat, second-hand leather breeches, a wig, a cap, boots, bag, shirts, night caps, pen and ink, sword, magnifying glass, spy-glass (telescope), a gauze veil (to protect head from midges), journal, paper, own works on birds and plants

Wildlife and wild weather

Throughout the expedition, Linnaeus gathered specimens of wildlife to take home. He was excited about the plants he discovered, especially the **lichens** and mosses that are common in Lapland. He wrote notes in his journal and drew pictures to record what he saw.

For the first part of the journey, Linnaeus went north to the city of Umeå. The journey was very hard. It took Linnaeus 11 days to cover what he estimated to be 644 kilometres, because the weather was so foggy and stormy.

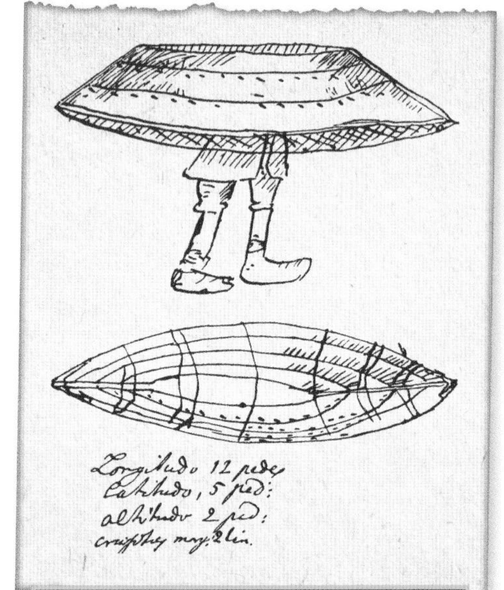

Linnaeus drew and wrote about all kinds of things in his journal. This picture shows a local guide carrying a boat on his head!

Linnaeus's 2,000-kilometre route

On the next part of his journey, Linnaeus headed northwest, away from the well-marked routes. Lots of rain made the trail and stony paths difficult. He was given shelter by a group of women who were looking after their sheep and goats. They gave him a dried and salted bird to eat, and a bed of reindeer hides to sleep in.

The weather continued to get worse, but Linnaeus plodded on. Soon the roads became too steep and muddy, and his horse kept stumbling. So Linnaeus had to hire a guide and get a boat to the town of Lycksele. The local pastor let him stay a few nights, before he set off into the land where the Sami lived.

Linnaeus and the Sami

The Sami people are the native people of Lapland. When Linnaeus spent time with them he observed them following herds of reindeer, which spend the winter in the lower forests, and the summer in the mountains. The Sami traditionally lived mainly on fish and the meat of reindeer. They used reindeer skins to make tents and clothes. Linnaeus was eager to see their customs and traditions. Like all explorers, he was curious, but this was also part of the scientific study he'd promised to the Royal Society of Uppsala in return for their grant.

Linnaeus drew pictures of the Sami's customs. For example, he watched how they built their tents. The tents were temporary because the Sami travelled with the reindeer.

Linnaeus noticed how healthy the Sami were. He thought of a number of reasons: pure air and pure water, no overeating, and peaceful minds as there was no squabbling or jealousy. All these things are still thought to be important for a healthy life.

An eventful trip

During Linnaeus's expedition to Lapland, he studied and made notes on the plants and birds he saw. He discovered at least a hundred new plants, and used his two-name system to name them. It was at this time that he worked out a similar system to name animals, too.

There were lots of high and low points in Linnaeus's journey through Lapland.

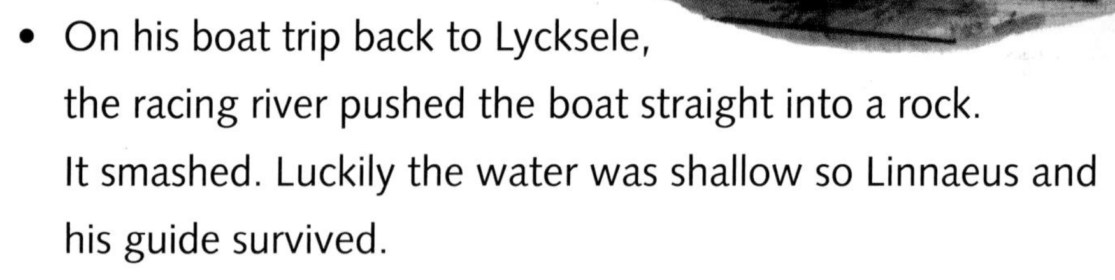

- Tired and hungry, the only food he was offered was "raw fish, whose mouths were full of worms". Fortunately he managed to buy some reindeer cheese instead.
- On his boat trip back to Lycksele, the racing river pushed the boat straight into a rock. It smashed. Luckily the water was shallow so Linnaeus and his guide survived.
- Travelling north, amongst many other flowers, he found a beautiful blood-red flower in the bog lands. He named it *Andromeda polifolia*, using his own two-name system.

- Near Tjamotis, Linnaeus saw the midnight sun – this far north, during some summer days, the sun never sets at all and it stays light all night. He described it as "not the least of Nature's miracles".

Linnaeus dressed in traditional Sami clothes

Back home – and away again

Back in Uppsala, Linnaeus added his Lapland finds to his natural history collection. He now had a huge collection of dead insects, pressed flowers and boxes of stones and shells. He worked hard on a book of Lapland flowers, his Botany lectures were still popular and he took on more teaching work. He also started working on a book classifying minerals. But he was always keen to travel – there were so many new plants, animals and rocks to discover.

Off to Dalarna

Just two years after his Lapland trip, in 1734, Linnaeus got the opportunity to lead an expedition to Dalarna, an area in central Sweden. Of course, he jumped at the chance to do some more exploring.

Linnaeus went with seven of the best medical students from Uppsala. They set off on horses for the 800-kilometre expedition. In the mountains, they studied the way people sometimes lived on very little – just lichen boiled in water and milk. Linnaeus and his companions explored the rocks, as he always hoped to find a valuable mineral or **ore**.

Linnaeus was so eager to order the world of minerals, he used the same system to class stones as he did for plants. He split them further into classes, general species and varieties. His stone classification method was so helpful to people, they used his method for the next 50 years. But then it was largely forgotten as **geologists** made new discoveries.

Love, a monster and lots of books

Linnaeus in love

In December 1734, Linnaeus went to spend Christmas with his friend Claes Sohlberg in the town of Falun. At a party, he met 18-year-old Sara Lisa Moraea, daughter of the town's physician. Linnaeus visited her a few times, once even dressed in Lapland clothes to impress her! They fell in love. Sara Lisa's father wasn't keen on her marrying a botanist who had little money. He finally agreed to let them marry, but first they had to wait three years. Perhaps he hoped Linnaeus would change career, or break off the engagement, during that time.

Linnaeus was now 27 years old and still a student, although he'd been lecturing and tutoring other students for the last five years! The lack of teaching and money, and Linnaeus's own interests, had stopped him finishing his degree.

Heading for Holland

Linnaeus's next trip was to Holland with his friend Claes in 1735. He could finally complete his degree in Holland, because lots of scholars of natural history lived there. Also, he wanted to see the rare plants in the well-known Botanical Garden in Amsterdam. Claes's father paid for the trip and offered Linnaeus a salary to teach Claes. Linnaeus was pleased.

Amsterdam Botanical Garden

Before leaving, Linnaeus wrote and sent a poem, called "A Lover's Farewell" to Sara Lisa, because he knew he'd be away for months. Just getting to Holland took Linnaeus and Claes a long time. They first travelled to Denmark, hoping for a ship to Holland. But after waiting five days, they decided to change routes, and take a ship to Germany instead. They knew they should be able to travel on to Holland from there.

Meeting a monster

While travelling through Germany, they stopped in Hamburg. Linnaeus explored bookshops and libraries. He was also taken to inspect a very strange, and famous, creature.

Linnaeus and the hydra

Everyone likes to see a monster. Today, people travel to Scotland from all round the world, hoping to see the Loch Ness Monster, but in Hamburg in Linnaeus's time, people went to see the "seven-headed hydra". It was just a stuffed creature, which now only exists in a drawing.

Linnaeus immediately knew it was a fake. He saw that the claws and jaws had come from weasels. The body was made of glued-on snakeskin scales. The stuffed animal had been stolen from the altar of a church during a battle in the 1600s. Linnaeus thought that perhaps monks at the church had made the hydra to represent the end of the world.

The owner of the hydra at the time was the burgomaster (chief magistrate) of Hamburg. The burgomaster was planning to sell it for a lot of money, but people soon lost interest when Linnaeus declared it a fake. Frightened that the burgomaster would be cross with him, Linnaeus quickly left Hamburg.

Becoming a doctor

As soon as he arrived in Holland, Linnaeus focused on finishing his medical degree. He wrote another thesis – this time on a disease called malaria.

Linnaeus and malaria

In the 18th century malaria was a common disease, but it was called "the ague". At the time, no one knew that mosquitoes passed the disease to people. Back in Uppsala University, Linnaeus had noticed that almost all the students suffered from malaria. He worked hard in Sweden to find out what caused it. At the time, people thought it was caused by getting cold, or eating certain foods. Linnaeus came up with a new idea, which was a step closer to the truth.

He found out that malaria was more common in areas with clay soil. He thought that clay got into the drinking water and caused the disease. In fact, clay soil with stagnant water is a great place for malaria mosquitoes to multiply and grow. So Linnaeus was right in one way. People are more likely to get malaria near areas of stagnant water. But he was wrong to think that the water itself caused the disease.

The cause of malaria was finally discovered in 1897. A British doctor called Ronald Ross saw that it was caused by tiny parasites that are passed into people by mosquito bites.

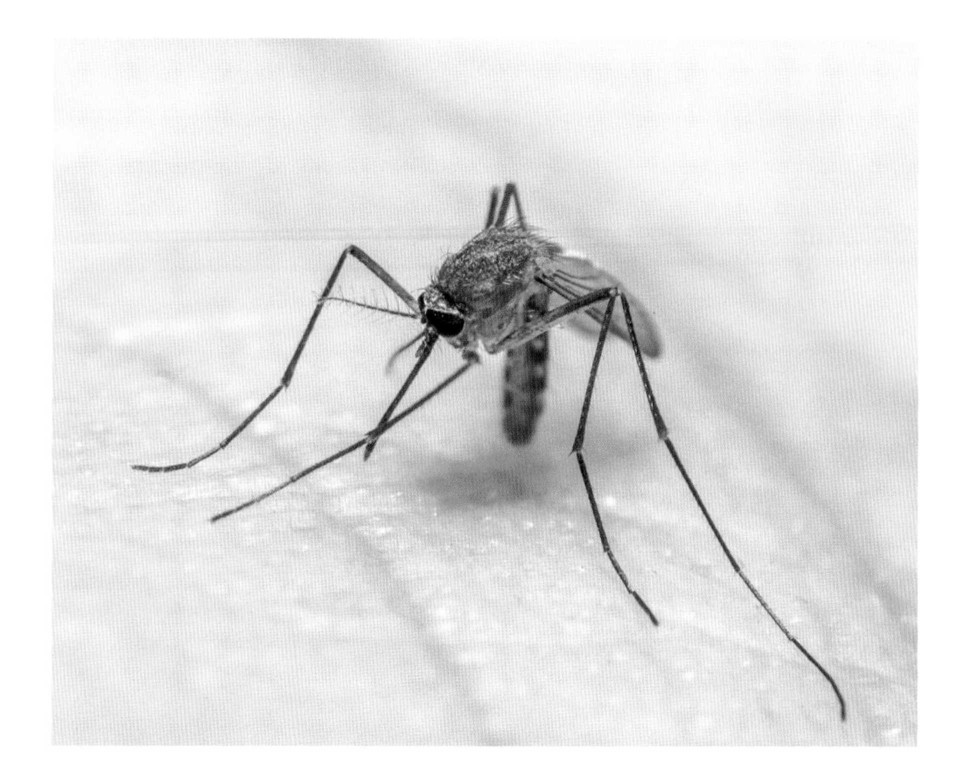

More study

Linnaeus was finally awarded his degree in Medicine in 1735 at a university near Amsterdam, nearly eight years after he first began studying Medicine. He carried on with his studies, and visited the botanical gardens in the cities of Amsterdam and Leiden.

Amsterdam Botanical Garden

These gardens were created in 1638, and were famous long before Linnaeus arrived in Holland. One amazing plant in the Amsterdam gardens is the Eastern Cape Giant Cycad from South Africa. This plant is still alive today. It's 300 years old and would have been there when Linnaeus visited the gardens.

Professor Burman was responsible for the Amsterdam Botanical Garden when Linnaeus visited. He challenged Linnaeus to identify a rare plant. Linnaeus examined it and tasted the leaves, and then named it. The director didn't agree at first, but more evidence proved Linnaeus right. The director was so impressed, he let Linnaeus live and work in his home. Also, he paid him to study some of the plants in the gardens.

Professor Johannes Burman

Catching up with an old friend

In Leiden, Linnaeus bumped into his old friend Peter Artedi. They renewed their decision to classify the whole of the plant and animal kingdoms. Six weeks later, Artedi fell into a canal in Amsterdam and drowned. Linnaeus was very upset and spent weeks finishing his friend's book on Artedi's main subject – fish. Linnaeus made sure it was published, too.

Linnaeus's most famous book

In Holland, Linnaeus worked hard on his own botanical books and papers. By the mid-1730s he was greatly admired by other professors. They helped him to publish his works. For example, in 1735, they paid to print the first edition of Linnaeus's now famous work *Systema Naturae,* which introduced his important classification system of the natural world. This edition only had 14 pages and is now very rare. Only 29 copies are known to exist, and they're very valuable.

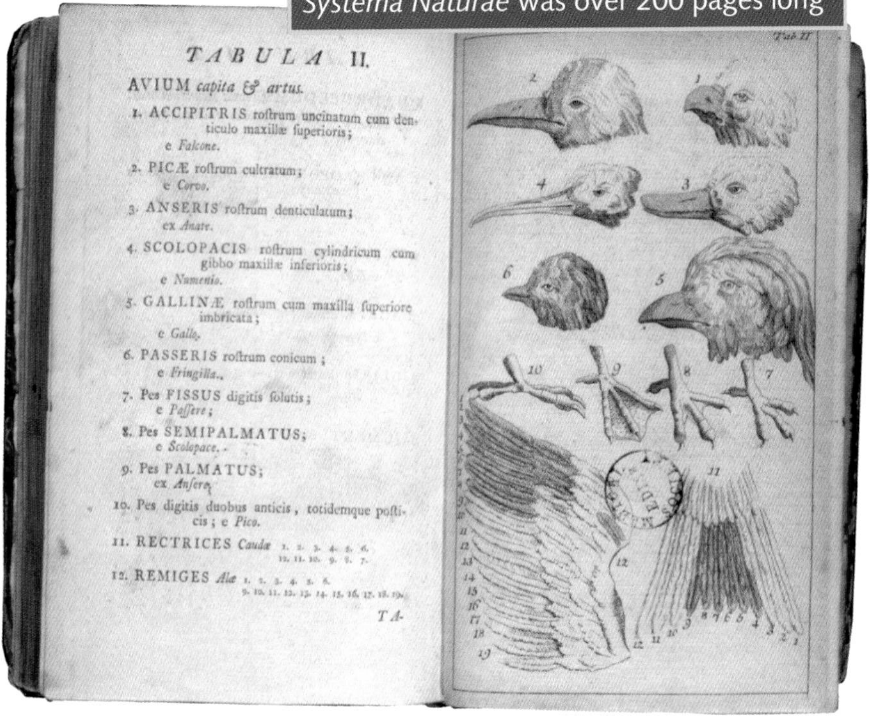

As Linnaeus classified more species, his books got longer. This 1756 edition of *Systema Naturae* was over 200 pages long

Linnaeus kept working on the book, adding more species of plants and animals, and types of minerals, so it got longer and longer. His classification system became more complicated too. He was the first to use the term *Mammalia*, meaning mammals. As more discoveries were made about animals, he moved many into the "mammal" class. For example, in the first edition of *Systema Naturae*, he classified whales as fish. Then in 1758 in the tenth edition, he correctly reclassified them as mammals. He was also the first to reclassify bats. Scientists had always classified them as birds, but Linnaeus classified them as mammals too.

In the tenth edition, he also used his two-word naming system for plants and animals throughout – the naming system we still use today. Between 1766 and 1768, the twelfth edition of *Systema Naturae* had grown to three volumes of 2,300 pages.

Linnaeus's dream job

George Clifford was a wealthy businessman, in charge of one of the biggest trading companies in the world: the Dutch East India Trading Company. The company brought important goods, like tea, from Asia to Europe.

Clifford had a big estate in Holland where he collected plants and animals from overseas. The zoo included tigers, apes, wild dogs and birds. In September 1735, Clifford asked Linnaeus to work on his estate, looking after the plants. Linnaeus was thrilled to live and work amongst the famous collection of living natural history. The only break he had from his job was a month's trip to England, to visit famous naturalists there, and see plant collections and libraries.

East India House in Amsterdam, headquarters of the East India Company

Growing bananas

Working for Clifford, Linnaeus quickly showed his knowledge of plants. For example, Clifford had a banana plant, but no one in Holland had been able to get a banana *flower* to grow, let alone a banana. But after only four months, Linnaeus succeeded in growing a banana flower. He did this by putting the plant in rich soil and letting it dry out. Next, he gave it masses of water, like the deluge of rain in a tropical storm. Botanists across Europe were amazed, and Linnaeus became even more famous. Later, Linnaeus even managed to get a banana to grow.

Medicines and marriage

Back to medicine again

In spring 1738, after three years away, Linnaeus decided he should go home to Sweden, because he'd heard that Sara Lisa was starting to see another man. Still believing in her loyalty, he didn't rush back, but stopped in France to meet important naturalists in Paris. When he got back to Falun to see her, they were formally engaged. Linnaeus was greatly admired by scientists abroad, but Sara Lisa's father didn't care about that. Before they could marry, Linnaeus had to have a stable career and be earning good money. So in 1738, he went to Stockholm and set himself up as a doctor.

Stockholm in the 1700s

Doctors and quacks

In the 1700s, the world of medicine was nothing like today. Knowledge was poor; for example, many thought disease was spread by gases in the air. Many doctors still believed in an ancient system of medicine, in which illnesses were blamed on an **imbalance** of four types of fluid in the body called "humors". Lots of the treatments used seem very bizarre today, such as cobweb pills for fevers, and pills of dried and powdered toad for asthma.

Surgery was still done in filthy conditions, there were no vaccinations, and medicines were usually made from plants, mixed by the doctors themselves or by people called apothecaries. Many so-called physicians, nicknamed "quacks", sold treatments for illnesses knowing they wouldn't work.

Improving medicine

Trained, professional doctors like Linnaeus were gradually separating themselves from these dishonest and usually uneducated people. For example, organisations were set up in Europe for trained doctors and surgeons. So the profession was becoming more respected. Eventually, rules were made to try to control who could give out medicine or medical advice. However, there were still plenty of quacks about, and patients often died. But slowly, through more careful research and observation of the human body, the world of medicine improved during Linnaeus's life.

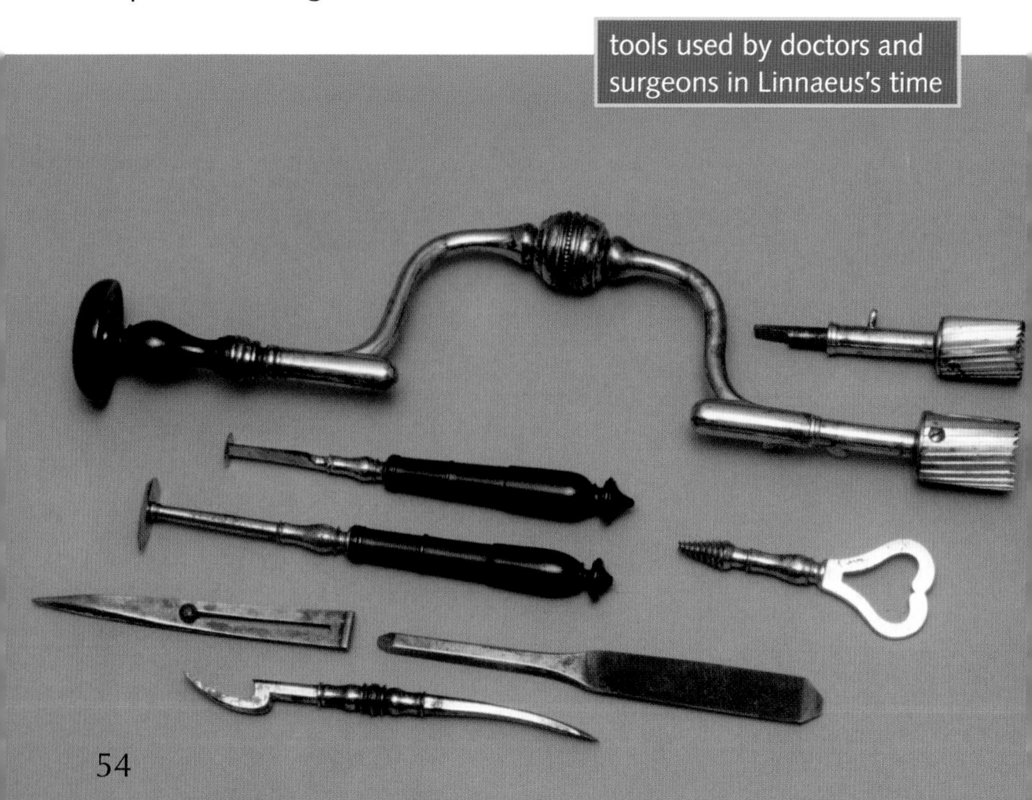

tools used by doctors and surgeons in Linnaeus's time

It was hardly surprising that people didn't trust Linnaeus when he set up as a young and inexperienced doctor. Linnaeus wrote jokingly that he couldn't even get a dog as a patient! He felt as if everyone was laughing at him now, in spite of all his hard work.

To find patients, he decided to go into taverns and coffee-houses where he might meet people. He found a patient with a serious disease and treated him with mercury. Even though mercury is a poisonous metal, it was a popular remedy at the time. Luckily for Linnaeus, his patient got better, and this success led to more patients. Soon he had 40 to 60 patients every day!

Nosology

Nosology has nothing to do with noses. It's the classification of diseases. Linnaeus devised his own nosology for diseases. By 1763, he'd put all diseases into 11 major groups, then into genera and species.

A *fashionable doctor*

Linnaeus's success came partly from seeking advice from other specialists. For example, he wrote to a doctor in France, whom he'd known for several years, asking for advice on practical treatments. Linnaeus was also a good observer, exploring the remedies that nature had to offer, and carefully observing their effects.

As Linnaeus's fame spread, more important and wealthy patients came to him for advice. One such patient was a Swedish senator's wife. He treated her cough with a sweet made from the sap of a Middle Eastern plant. It worked, and she recommended Linnaeus to the queen of Sweden. Soon he was treating the royal family.

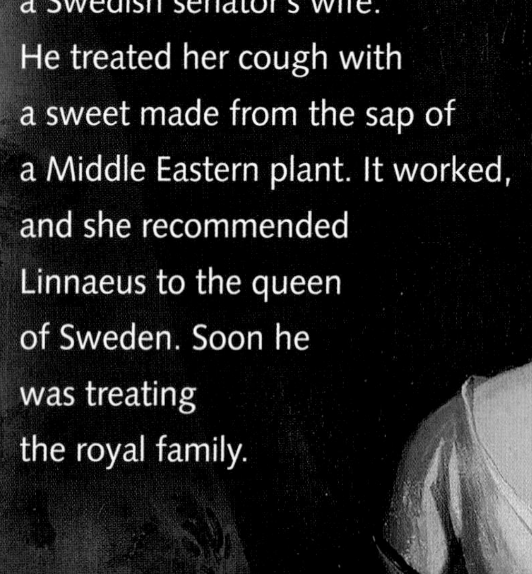

Ulrika Eleonora, Queen of Sweden

Linnaeus's medicines

Linnaeus grew his own plants for medicine, including the ones shown here.

Linnaeus called these poppies *Papaver somniferum* ("somniferum" means "sleepy"). He knew that their juice made people sleepy. Today, it's called opium and is known to be very dangerous. A form of it is still used as a painkiller called morphine.

Linnaeus used this plant, valerian, for different things, including to relax people, and to treat worms in the intestines. Today, it's taken as a herbal medicine to help people relax.

Lots of Linnaeus's plants had been used as medicines for hundreds of years. Chamomile was used by the ancient Greeks to help heal wounds, and make them less red and sore.

Linnaeus put together a book of plants, animals and minerals used as medicines. His book *Materia Medica* – which means "medicine" – was published in 1749, and was used across Europe for decades.

Rich and famous

By 1739, Linnaeus was making plenty of money, so Sara Lisa's father let them get married that June. After a month's honeymoon, Linnaeus had to go back to Stockholm as he was so busy with work. He wasn't able to set up a comfortable family home until October 1741, so until then Linnaeus and his wife spent much of the time apart, with Sara Lisa still living near Falun. Linnaeus often seemed more focused on his work than his marriage. He didn't even visit his wife when their son, Carl, was born in January 1741. Many people would describe him as a workaholic – always putting his work first.

In fact, in 1741, Linnaeus went on another adventure. People high up in the Swedish authorities invited him to go on an expedition to the Swedish islands of Öland and Gotland, to search for valuable natural resources, such as plants for dye and clay soil for making pottery. Sweden was a poor country so natural resources were important.

Falun
Uppsala
Stockholm
Gotland
Sweden
Öland

On the islands, Linnaeus found a new crop plant, hayseed, which was so valuable it paid for the costs of his expedition. But what thrilled him most were the wild orchids that grew in Öland. People still go to see these beautiful wild orchids today. He wrote about his expedition in *Öland and Gotland Journey*. It was the first book he wrote in Swedish and not Latin. He wanted ordinary people, who couldn't read Latin, to enjoy it – which they still do today.

Fame

Family life

In October 1741, Linnaeus took a new job as Professor of Medicine and Botany at Uppsala University, and moved with his family to Uppsala. They lived in a house in the grounds of the university's botanical garden. The garden had been neglected, but Linnaeus soon planted new flowers and had new greenhouses and a tropical hothouse built.

As well as new plants, he collected living animals never seen in Sweden before, including a cockatoo, parrots, an orangutan and goldfish. Most were bought with grants from abroad, and a pupil from England gave him the goldfish and orangutan.

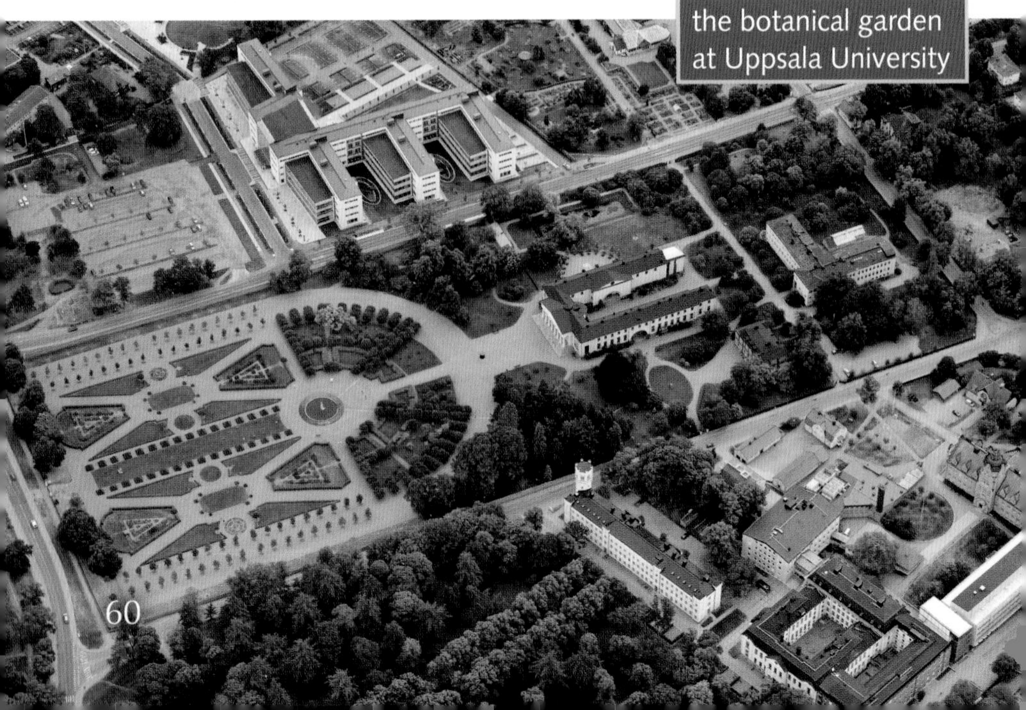

the botanical garden at Uppsala University

Linnaeus had a parrot that sat on his shoulder, which called "Come in!" to knocking visitors. He also taught it to squawk "Blow your nose!" to one of the gardeners.

Linnaeus was sometimes given creatures by the king and queen of Sweden. One of these was a North American animal the size of a badger. Linnaeus had never seen such a creature before. He described how the animal's "long snout" gave it a good sense of smell. If there was cake on the table, the creature was "on it in a flash" even though it was blind. Linnaeus tried feeding it a strange range of things, and found it most disliked sauerkraut (pickled vegetables) or raw or boiled fish. We know now that the animal was a racoon.

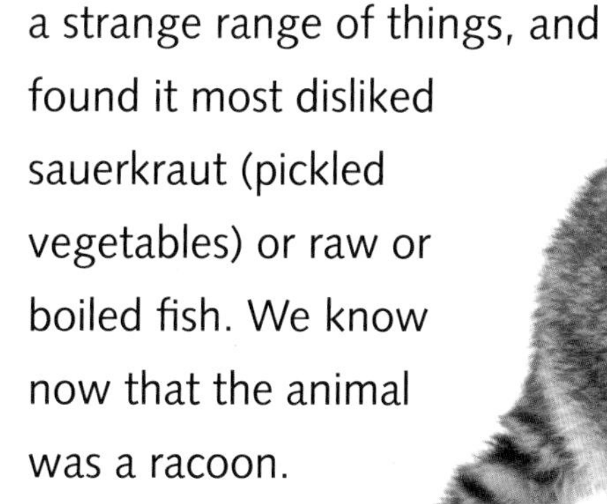

Linnaeus the teacher

Linnaeus lectured on Botany as well as Medicine and was a very popular lecturer. He took crowds of 150 students on weekly trips into the countryside. The students who found the most interesting plants or creatures won the prize of having lunch with Linnaeus. The excited crowd marched home from the countryside expeditions, banging drums and shouting, "Long live Linnaeus!"

In his role as Professor of Medicine and Botany, Linnaeus had ideas about diet and how to lead a healthy life. Some of Linnaeus's ideas were based on superstition rather than science. For example, he believed:

- you shouldn't rock babies, as it would make them vomit;
- draughts cling to walls, so you should put your bed in the middle of a room;

Linnaeus and his wife Sara Lisa in the botanical garden at Uppsala

- mutton is the best meat for people who don't do physical work;
- brown and reddish cows produce the best milk.

Many of his other ideas are still valid today, and he was good at persuading his students that his ideas and arguments were right. Students remembered his lectures because they were both fascinating and entertaining. Linnaeus had a good sense of humour and was able to make students roar with laughter.

During this time in Uppsala, Linnaeus was a happy man. He was famous, earned good money, had a growing family with more children and was working mainly on the subject he loved – botany.

Linnaeus and the "apostles"

Some of Linnaeus's students were called his "apostles" because they admired him so much. He sent them on expeditions to collect plants from other countries. For example, some apostles went off to bring back tea plants. Linnaeus knew China made a lot of money growing and selling tea, so he thought perhaps Sweden could do the same. However, things didn't go entirely to plan. One apostle was ready to bring a tea plant back but it fell off the side of his ship. Another apostle's plant withered and died during the voyage home. When Linnaeus finally got some tea plants, even *he* couldn't get them to survive in the Swedish climate.

Many of the plant samples that apostles brought back were added to Linnaeus's collection. One apostle alone brought back 90 North American plants.

As Linnaeus's students travelled abroad, they spread the use of Linnaeus's two-word naming system. In 1786, one of his cleverest students, Daniel Solander, went on board Captain Cook's ship the *Endeavour*, and took part in Cook's voyage to south-eastern Australia. It was a voyage into the unknown, because no European had visited this part of the world before.

Daniel Solander

Solander worked with another botanist, called Joseph Banks, on this and other voyages, also visiting Iceland and Scotland's Hebrides and Orkney islands. Together, they gathered about 30,000 new plant species.

Joseph Banks

A hectic life

While his apostles were off around the world, Linnaeus was increasingly busy in Uppsala. He and Sara Lisa had seven children in all, but despite his growing family, Linnaeus was focused on teaching and writing. He wrote lots of books and papers about fossils and rocks, and all kinds of creatures, from Tree Boa snakes to glowing grasshoppers. All Linnaeus's projects took masses of work. His book *Species Plantarum* (1753) listed every plant he knew: 5,900 species. This book finally persuaded other scientists to accept his two-word naming system and they no longer called plants by the older, longer names.

Growing pearls

Pearls were very valuable, and Linnaeus was a bit short of money after buying the family a holiday home in the country. So he studied mussel pearls and decided to try to make some himself. If it worked, he hoped to sell his idea for money.

Linnaeus knew that pearls formed round something inside the mussel shell, such as a grain of sand. He bored holes into mussel shells and put a tiny bit of plaster or limestone inside on a wire. Then he put the mussels back in a river. The experiment was a success! After five or six years, pea-sized pearls grew. In 1761, he received money from the government for his idea.

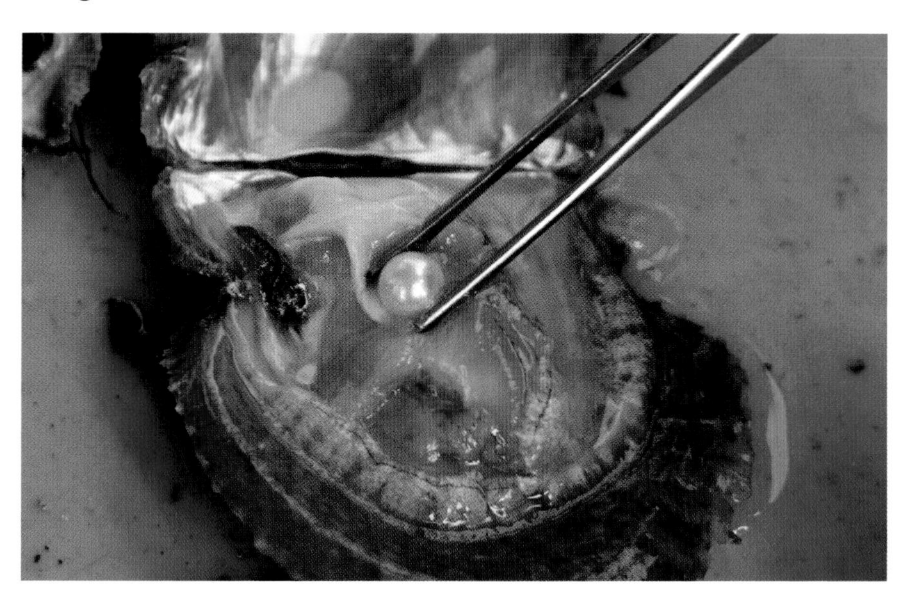

Important friends

In the 1750s, having been their doctor for some time, Linnaeus became friends with the new king and queen of Sweden. At the time, the monarchy was becoming less powerful in Sweden, but the king and queen were still wealthy and important. It was fashionable for wealthy people to have natural history collections and Linnaeus had been writing a catalogue for the king's collection, which was mainly preserved animals in jars, stuffed birds and insects. In 1751, Linnaeus was called to the royal palace to catalogue the queen's collection of dead butterflies and insects, too.

King Adolf Frederick of Sweden

Queen Louisa Ulrika

The queen found him witty and entertaining. He walked with the king every evening and even played a party game in court with them both. It was Blind Man's Bluff, where – blindfolded – one person has to catch another player. He peeped out of his blindfold and deliberately caught the queen. No one else dared to do such a thing.

By 1757, Linnaeus and his work were so respected that he'd gained many awards, and had even been knighted in 1755. Botanists were using his plant names, and he'd further developed his classification systems. People praised his many books and papers. Scientific societies and academies all around the world offered Linnaeus membership.

When Linnaeus became very ill in his sixties, he still worked hard. But after Linnaeus had a **stroke**, he couldn't speak properly. The king visited him and cheered him up with a gift of 16 chests of plants. Linnaeus was also pleased to hear how the royal gardens in France and England were using his two-word naming system to label their plants. By now he was admired by lots of important foreign writers, such as the German writer and statesman, Goethe. Linnaeus was delighted when an admiring letter from the philosopher Rousseau arrived, saying he'd read Linnaeus's works and thought them far more important than so many other books he'd studied.

Linnaeus was seen across Europe as one of the most important natural scientists in the world. His love of nature had inspired readers in and beyond Sweden. He'd opened people's eyes to nature so they saw it in new ways.

Linnaeus died in January 1778. He'd wanted to be buried near his country summer home, but he was too important to Sweden and the world of science for that. His funeral was in Uppsala Cathedral. It was a huge state ceremony, and crowds lined the streets to pay their respects. A medallion was placed near his grave in Uppsala Cathedral with the Latin words *Princeps Botanicorum*, which means "Prince of Botany".

Linnaeus's desk at Uppsala

Linnaeus's legacy

Today, Linnaeus is still admired all around the world. His name is remembered in lots of ways.

- In London, every year, a Linnean Medal is given to an outstanding biologist.
- In 2010, Linnaeus University, in Växjö and Kalmar, Sweden, was named after him.
- There's even a crater on the moon named after Linnaeus – the Linné Crater.

Linnaeus's two-word system for naming plants and animals is still used today, and we also still use something like Linnaeus's system of ranks to organise animals, from kingdoms to classes to genres to species. Other ranks have been added to those Linnaeus used, as our scientific knowledge of animals has increased over time.

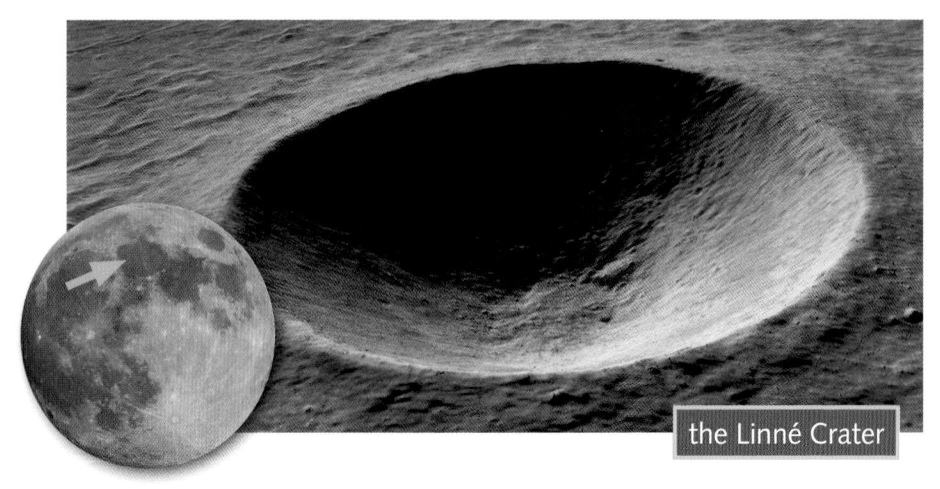

the Linné Crater

Linnaeus's work in taxonomy has helped scientists all over the world to identify animals and plants and to share their knowledge. For example, the naturalist and TV presenter Sir David Attenborough found Linnaeus's system of two-word Latin names useful when exploring a forest in Borneo. Neither Attenborough nor his guide could understand each other's language. In the forest, Attenborough heard a bird call, put his hand to his ear and looked at his guide. His guide said, "*Caprimulgus macrurus*", which Attenborough immediately understood. It was the Latin name for the large-tailed nightjar.

Linnaeus's impact on science

Linnaeus's work influenced many important scientists who came after him – including Charles Darwin and George Mendel, who worked on **evolution** and **heredity**.

Linnaeus and Darwin

Linnaeus's work had a direct effect on Charles Darwin's theory of evolution. Linnaeus had hoped that it would be possible to name every plant and animal that existed, but Darwin's work eventually showed that this would be impossible. Darwin's theory was set out in his book, *On the Origin of Species*, in 1859. He explained that species develop, or evolve, over time. So the living world does not remain static. It can never be listed in a book. Darwin also proved how natural living things are related in subtler ways than, for example, the number of stamens a plant has. This led to the development of a more complicated but more accurate classification system of both animals and plants.

Charles Darwin

Linnaeus and Mendel

Linnaeus discovered how different types of plant might together form a new species of plant through a process called hybridisation. From around the 1850s, George Mendel went on to use this knowledge to grow different types of pea plants. Mendel's work was important as he discovered some of the rules of heredity – how features of a parent plant are passed to its younger plants, just as a child might inherit brown eyes from a parent.

Linnaeus will always be remembered as an explorer, too. Not only did he search for new types of plants in distant places, he also started the idea of travelling far away to gather specimens for study. His students were the first to go on expeditions to explore the natural world. Since then, generations of scientists have gone on similar expeditions, discovering thousands more types of plants and animals.

George Mendel

Glossary

botanical garden	a garden with rare or interesting plants from around the world
botanist	someone who studies plants
botany	the science of plants
classification	arranging animals and plants in groups according to their similarities
commonplace	everyday, usual
dean	a senior priest
evolution	the process by which different kinds of living things develop and change over time
geologists	people who study what the earth is made of and how it was formed
heredity	the way in which characteristics (such as eye colour or leaf shape) are passed from parent animals and plants to their offspring
imbalance	when things are out of balance or out of proportion
lichens	simple, slow-growing plants that grow on rocks and trees
minerals	substances that are formed naturally under the ground
natural history	the scientific study of animals and plants, based on observing them
nomadic	wandering, with no fixed living place
ore	a solid material found in the ground, from which you can get a valuable metal or mineral
pollination	the way in which pollen is transferred to the female reproductive parts of a plant, so fruit and seeds can be formed

stroke	when brain cells die because the flow of blood to the brain has been interrupted or reduced
Theology	the study of religious belief
thesis	a long essay written as part of a university degree
turf	grass and the top layer of earth held together by the roots of the grass

Index

Linnaeus timeline

May 1707: born in Råshult, southern Sweden

1709: family moves to Stenbrohult

1717: goes to school in Växjö

1727: leaves school and goes to Lund University

1729: moves to Uppsala University

1730: develops own system for classifying plants and animals

1732: trip to Lapland

1734: trip to Dalarna

1734: meets Sara Lisa Moraea

1735: goes to Holland and finishes medical degree

1735: *Systema Naturae* (first edition) published

1735: works on George Clifford's estate

1738: returns to Sweden and begins work as a doctor

1739: marries Sara Lisa Moraea

1741: trip to Öland and Gotland

1741: moves with family to Uppsala

1753: *Species Plantarum* published

1755: receives a knighthood

1778: dies and is buried in Uppsala Cathedral

Ideas for reading

Written by Clare Dowdall, PhD
Lecturer and Primary Literacy Consultant

Reading objectives:

- discuss understanding and explore the meaning of words in context
- draw inferences and justify these with evidence
- explain and discuss their understanding of what they have read, including through formal presentations and debates, maintaining a focus on the topic and using notes where necessary

Spoken language objectives:

- participate in discussions, presentations, performances, role play, improvisations and debates

Curriculum links: Science – living things and their habitats

Resources: ICT, paper and pens, whiteboards

Build a context for reading

- Ask children to name someone who has influenced them – a good or bad influence. Discuss what being "influential" means.
- Look at the cover and read the blurb. Ask if anyone has heard of Carl Linnaeus, and for ideas about other known people who work in this field (Sir David Attenborough).
- Challenge children to suggest how animals and plants can be classified into different groups and help them to understand that classifying is a way of sorting things according to their characteristics.

Understand and apply reading strategies

- Ask children to read pp2–3 with a partner, noting as many facts that are given and that can be deduced about Linnaeus on a whiteboard (he was a taxonomist, intelligent etc.)
- Ask children to highlight the given facts, and their deductions in two different colours. Discuss how their deductions have been made using contextual information – and how this strategy can help us make meaning.